HUNGER AND PREDATION
POOJA MITTAL BISWAS

Other publications by Pooja Mittal Biswas

POETRY
Diaries of a Marked Man
Musings on Poetry
Subliminal Dust

NON-FICTION
A Diasporic Mythography: Myth, Legend and Memory
  in the Literature of the Indian Diaspora
Gendering Time, Timing Gender: The Deconstruction
  of Gender in Time Travel Fiction

FICTION
Earthstone
Strange Fires

HUNGER

AND

PREDATION

POOJA MITTAL BISWAS

BOOK 04

SERIES 5

CORDITE
BOOKS

First printed in 2023
by Cordite Publishing Inc.

PO Box 58
Castlemaine 3450
Victoria, Australia
cordite.org.au | corditebooks.org.au

National Library of Australia
Cataloguing-in-Publication:

Biswas, Pooja Mittal
Hunger and Predation
978-0-6489176-9-4 paperback
I. Title.
A821.3

Poetry set in Rabenau 10 / 15
Cover design by Zoë Sadokierski
Text design by Kent MacCarter and Zoë Sadokierski
Printed and bound by McPherson's Printing, Maryborough, Victoria.

10 9 8 7 6 5 4 3 2 1

CONTENTS

PREFACE xi

INTRODUCTION xii

to Miranda, from Caliban 1

Western Sydney fugue: Parramatta 2

audition no. 5 5

hir 7

anatomy of an orgasm 9

on the occasion of your wedding 12

the taxidermist 16

the M word 18

marine 19

conversation with gods 1 20

Western Sydney fugue: Harris Park 22

like the boys do 24

immunity 28

strobe lights 29

garlands 30

first blood 33

s/he 34

vespertine 36

Western Sydney fugue: Blacktown 38

Quetzalcoatl 39

glitch 40

bandu, sakha   42

swim   45

on madness   46

conversation with gods 2   62

alias   65

Western Sydney fugue: Glenwood   66

ACKNOWLEDGEMENTS   69

PREFACE

As written by the author, age 12.

The wolf came to visit her one night, just as she was going to sleep. He crawled in beside her in the shallow neck of their cave, and the night was a thin black sheet she pulled over them both.

He was close and warm and smelled of blood. She lit a match he did not flinch away from, and in the faint light she saw his jaws part and saw that they were dotted with red. A soft tuft of feathers was ridiculous between his teeth.

'Another sparrow?' she asked, but the wolf only tilted his head. His teeth gleamed, gently, and she reached into the wolf's wet mouth to pluck the feathers out. One by one.

His long, strange tongue came out to lap at her wrist.

'How was the bird?' she murmured afterwards, when his jaws were clean and he rested his heavy head on her shoulder, huffing in satisfaction.

'Light,' he said. 'Such a light thing.'

'Best get you something heavier, then.'

The wolf glanced up at her, for an instant, as though startled. His belly was warm and furred against hers, moving with each breath. His paws were quiet.

'Yes,' he said eventually, and her fingers stroked his coat until he sighed. 'Yes.'

INTRODUCTION

In this fifth book of poetry, Pooja Mittal Biswas's voice achieves musicality. While strong themes lend coherence to the whole, the language cascades and moves forward with an inner force.

The collection's second poem is in the voice of a pregnant Indian woman with a panoptic view of immigrants in Australia. It defines hunger as the hunger for freedom 'to be, to be allowed to be, untouched and uncontained, spoken and heard', and it ends with the resolve that 'my child will speak.' We quickly discover that this child, or childlike voice, is the poet herself, as she pores over memories, including those traumatic, to locate herself.

Biswas considers Nigeria her first country; however, in *Hunger and Predation*, she sets claim to her heritage as Indian. She conducts a dialogue with this Indianness, drawing from it as well as not fitting into its framework. She comments on the restrictive social mores that deny selfhood – 'a ghost like all women are urged to become.' By contrast, her own passions are blatant ('a wolf hiding in the tall grass').

Biswas uses Indian vocabulary with ease, importing her immigrant voice into Australian literature. Interior monologues with the gods of Indian mythology have a freshness and clear vision that can only come from a distance.

A second theme of this book is gender queerness, which is interrogated as Biswas works through a sense of being 'agender.' The yearning to be free of categorisations goes along with the assertion that she is much more than identity. In the poem 'hir' she writes 'of gendered traits, a cartography of the mind that history has mapped onto people as borders are onto nations.' In another poem, 'anatomy of an orgasm', she notes the dissonance – 'the wiring's off.' In 'glitch' she writes – '& I ask myself one thousand times an afternoon/whether the way I perform gender/ is artificial or the real thing.' 'Immunity' articulates the horror of having been sexually abused in childhood.

Whereas confessional poetry can deteriorate into fetishism, in Biswas's hands the first person narrative soars – detailed, raw, palpable, her poems have a sense of immediacy.

Hunger and Predation ends with a transported long poem titled 'madness' that more than hints at the poet's mental state and therapy. Stunned, I found myself anxious for the poet – so human is this book, her hunger and predation included.

—Mani Rao

to Miranda, from Caliban

I want to eat you, darling bear, little flower.
the soft, singular meat of an armpit.
the back of the knee. your foot.

oh, thou comport a hymn to symmetry.
the little bones, xylophones
on which I tap
my music. the isle is full
of noises, but you
are its most beautiful.

pretty, I will make you a noise.
I will make of you
    a twangling
        instrument.

Western Sydney fugue: Parramatta

childbirth is as bloody as war & as I am
due to give birth soon, I too will be reborn
as a mother, an Indian mother, an Australian.
there are weights attached to me that drag my limbs under.
in every place I've been is every other place I've been.
we immigrants live out of boxes
in our heads even after
we've unpacked the ones in our garages. I was born
in a hospital south of Murtala Mohammed Airport in Lagos, Nigeria
but I find traces of there in Parramatta, where
I teach when I'm in
my eighth month of pregnancy. there are many of us here,
Sudanese, Indian, Nigerian, Pakistani, Lebanese, Iranian,
Malaysian, Sri Lankan, Filipina. my students come from homes
where the parents watch
Beverley Hills Cop
with Tamil subtitles & their children
watch Tamil movies with English subtitles. within the older boys
boils a khoon-red rage
emasculated
by otherness, by lessness, by being labelled
for every step they take, every curse they speak,
the intonations of their words, their gestures. allowed none
of the invisible liberties
white boys enjoy. within the girls & the women is a silt-dark
hunger to *be*, to be allowed to be, untouched & uncontained,
spoken & heard,
heard, heard, *heard.*
charred
dust & ants in the cracks
of our mouths. our blackness, our brownness, washed
up on the sugary shores of a country where

the hospitals aren't clogged like
sclerotic arteries, tiles slick with piss & vomit,
where the people aren't bled like cows
for sacrifice. we are seeking shelter. our organs
congeal outside of us, pumping, pulsing, vulnerable
to the knife-like questions we are asked:
where do you come from? when will you go back?
some of us have no choice but to stay.
our brothers, our sisters
in detention centres & we outside of them with survivors' guilt
worrying at us like a hangnail. we are doctors, labourers.
we are farmers whose bamboos & VCRs burned, whose crops
succumbed to war
& drought. we are artists who bleed net to canvas
& lovers who flee beheadings because our bodies happen
to be the same sex. we push & push, birthing a tomorrow
that never arrives. an unending, wracking labour.
when I think about giving birth in flight, I consider Blacktown Hospital
because I live there, but am advised by a local obstetrician
to opt for Norwest instead. I am upper-middle-class,
with private health insurance. I can afford it,
despite my colour, despite having been
born across the seas myself, in a hospital where my mother lay
sick & haemorrhaging on an unwashed bed
& nearly did not survive me.
now, my mother puts betel leaves in my mouth
for luck. my child squirms within my belly. across
Parramatta the train track is a dark vein,
needle-pricked, inflamed.
there are nerves that spark between the bones of this
place, its vertebrae of concrete & eyes of pebblecrete.
the shops, the smoked lungs of its body

& the streets, wan ribs creaking under the weight
they bear. the heavy quietude of a train
station at sunrise
      is an unborn child, a conglomeration
of our silenced words, our terrors, our hopes. I lull asleep
   to the rhythmic genome of that semi-silence, my hand curled
atop my swollen abdomen.
        my child, I decide, *my child will speak.*

audition no. 5

... cut! cut! cut!

blades that are fingers, & between the fingers,
     blades in the grass that

... cut! cut! cut!

the director is a diamond, dwindling.
sand fills the mossy gullies
where sea had been. the reel blacks out. under the crow's brow
is a single opal for an eye, a spear, an arrow. a brown woman
wanders onto stage right
as if lost,
    tissue
      or an apparatus
of bone & metal. tinsel drapes her legs.
she is a lit match. from her throat emerges
    a glorious plume of purple-blue fire
like the ocean at twilight, like what Lata Mangeshkar could make.
    there is a ship in her, too, a journey, a macabre
toy shelf of anthems & glued-together lighters & cigarettes,
      blood in her mouth
because the song cuts her as it escapes
into a lifeboat. the grips pour gasoline
    down her gullet & ignite her.
she never asked to be incandescent.
to be alight & radiant comes with a cost. the director contemplates

her shapes, her shadows
as one does a candle at vipassanā. he directs her fingers backward
until they snap, like her uncle used to, *good girl, good girl.* the waiting
    maw, the baring of teeth.

                    ... cut! cut! cut!

    she is as silent as all flames are. until
she's not, but who would sing if it burned them
to ashes? who would sing if the song slit them
    from glottis to belly? like the maach
her mother trained her to cook, to rub with spice
until her hands stung. hers is a skin of knives,
        of runes & hexes invisible
beneath the dermis. she is a churail. though dark, she is whitened
by ash & naked, like Kali, & when she dances, the world
    burns
            or maybe she does. there is
        no difference.

hir

being embodied
is the opposite of being trans-bodied,
gender a sequential pattern of dim/bright/dim/bright/dim/bright
like the passing of a train
on which you are not a passenger.

maroon & stalwart, the rednesses & brownnesses
sewn into undercarriages of blame
that curve inward, mouths of whales, rotating
Jonah in the belly of darkness

finding hir own shape.
rescued from kiln is clay, glazed & fired
into a bird with canine jaws, cracked but ruthlessly freed
from the prison of the flesh — the hips, the breasts. the vulva.

the penis, some strange protuberance
of gendered traits, a cartography of the mind
that history has mapped
onto people as borders are onto nations. imaginary

but warred over, killed for. we are kernels
of violent light
to keep us from
being discovered, being culled. allies,

we have not earned this violence.
it is injected, ink into imaginary veins,
& fashioned into new signatures for us to let
out in a blood contract of identity

until our lease expires. we are reduced to borrowers
of our bodies,
breasts bound or unbound, stubble shaved or un-,
stockings, glitter, corsets, cocks,

laughter in a parked Volvo
after midnight. we are brighter than we are
allowed, more ferocious, tiger-striped & hungry for the songs
of jungle birds.

from the subterranean loam in which we have been buried,
gathering nourishment from its tenebrous depths,
we will sing in a great flowering, a hurricane of springs.
so until then, we remain

a crust of barnacles on the hull of a ship,
glimmering and underwater.
seen only by skin divers
for pearls.

anatomy of an orgasm

genderqueer? gender? queer? nobody
    wants to hear
about my dream-self sloughing
my body off like snakeskin,
leaving only a crystalline,
    crepuscular sheathe
  on which marks of my
slow undulations remain.

no, they simply want
to hear about my vagina, about
its gnawing frustration
of not being able to orgasm
because it never feels quite *right*,
never feels quite *mine*, because
the wiring's off between there & here,
& my brain keeps expecting me to have
    a penis where
        there isn't one.
           cognitive   dissonance.
        a phantom limb.

yet, still I dream about you, about your waters
lapping at the red silt of my riverbed,
    formless but no less powerful for it.
      your undertow carries me out
    to sea where all things are strange
& I am no stranger than them, creatures
      alien to us both
floating past us in the depths, luminous
& translucent, their glowing limbs
extended trustingly into the black.

we swim by the light
of underwater volcanoes, their fire
blooming crimson
in the dark, sea anemones
of magma welling blood-like
from the earth. in that
slow welling is my pleasure, rare
as a flame lily & just as dangerous,
a velvet made of deeps
& lined with
teeth.

there, subterranean & inescapable,
an orgasm gathers at my root
like a storm of fireflies,
of needle-sharp stings upon my flesh:
a full-body flush,
a liquefying fever,
a rainfall of molten wax
dissolving my skin & leaving
nothing but a shudder
behind.

how do I explain
that I'm not so much coming
as *arriving*, reaching someplace,
going someplace, embodying someplace,
finger in the socket
afire with electricity.
as an agender asexual, I may be
a foreigner to this postcode, but nonetheless
I journey through it, a pilgrim

with half-formed feet, an excruciating
progress through unfamiliar
 terrain. hot sands & vines.

        but your ranges
are as familiar to me as my own are
not, & I chart the starlit, sun-hewed expanse
    of you, deserts to foothills,
with a worshipful mouth
where midnight-blue meets lavender:
that, *that* kiss.
        & once you cup my face & look
into my want as if into a dream, my body
remembers itself, shudders back to life
& its heat unspools
    like a golden tendon
        around my belly.
we hunt rabbits

    across corn fields,
darting in & out of sight between
the long grasses, mouths missing
each other mid-kiss, skidding & slick
as feet on wet cobblestones. but then
    you catch me & you
                lift us
                    & your
gulfstream fills my wet kite & soars
        & in the mad rush of an updraft
roaring in my ears like a thousand waterfalls
        I forget my body
            is not my own.

on the occasion of your wedding

yellow   saffron
    white   dill
your palm as intricately
lined with mehendi
    as the veins of
the banana leaf on which
    you offer up sacrifices
to the gods: a spoonful of kheer,
five fruits glistening like tongues,
    orange marigolds
        pink frangipani
a peda made of burnt flour & milk,
    sindoor
        turmeric
          dahi.

you are fragrant with jasmine
      henna
    & clean sweat
in damp silk, scents he will unfurl
    later tonight.
        the red gauze of
your sari is made opaque
    by how it drapes you,
its layers a lotus
of a thousand petals:
    the burden of beauty

yours to carry, as always.
your feet in gold-threaded slippers
   walk around the fire
with him
      seven clean times
         for the seven lives
you will live together.
   I stand behind your relatives
my hand full of hard
   prickles of uncooked rice,
my knuckles gripping
my own offering to
bless your
     union.

your head is bowed
      as if in shame
or submission, & you
follow his footsteps around
     the fire
as a good wife should, always
   following, never leading.

but there was once a fire between us,
no leading, no following, just one girl
& one monstrous almost-girl
pressed together in the shadows
   of Lodhi Park,
mouths open like night phlox
under the swaying

branches
        a pillar concealing us
from the eyes of all but gods.
did they see us, then? did they
        witness us as they witness
you now, & know
that what you are doing
        is a lie? maya
deceives us, its fabric
as opaque-yet-transparent as your sari,
        & can I blame you
when gods themselves
have woven the world with falsehoods
as carefully as they have embroidered
the gilt strands upon your sandals?

        does it matter
                that they are not true?

                they are
                        beautiful.

                        like
                                you.

shimmer-white   sunlit

                        your scarlet veil

your pursed mouth
your mouth
your mouth
your mouth.

he will keep you for seven
        lifetimes but I had you
for an eternity, twined upon a jute mat that left us
            bruised.
I had you for the long, starless centuries
before dawn, those unmeasured & infinite hours
        of thirsting & slaking
under a thick, stiff blanket.

let him
            have you now.
I
        had you first.

    & if eternity

            never ends

        then I will have you

        always.

the taxidermist

a pinned bird with stiff wings
      of lacquered wax, its iridescent blue plumage
giving way to the neat cut down its gut:
      the flower-bright blossoming
of a heart offered up
      by a smashed ribcage. the ribs are matchstick-fine,
delicate crowns, the heart a jewel-red kernel of sun ablaze
      under my scalpel. glossy pink viscera
the exact texture of your lips – I remember
      the sheen & the give of them,
a soft soft sheen, satiny & damning. your urn brims
with ashes like a cave does with patience. in my mirror
      your reflection mimics mine, but not;
your shape is mine yet skewed, a photo taken from an angle,
elongated, strange. a mockery, a caress. like all your touches were.
      I drink wine from your cuts. your blood

tastes like the moon. in the pale shavings of dawn drifting down
      from a chipped ceiling lies a sleeping wolf
beside its waking brother, through whose eyes I watch
      the night fade as pigment does.
I love you as wolves love the moon, as fate loves time, inevitable.
I want the water of you, the warp & the weft, the hip & thigh,
the weight of the breast. from the quiet forest
      behind you, you emerge:
your silver fur lovely & startling. you have a shard
of human husk left, just the one, stuck on your hindlimb.

      you are a wolf

like me. we form, re-form. meld.
our bodies merge. our claws, our fangs. a symphony of baying.
in my lab, light refracts through a plastic vase by the window.
the surface of the mirror gathers you
just beneath its skin of glass. you are coming out,
I am going in. or vice-versa. somewhere
we meet. your feet are mine, my jaws are not quite
yours. you are my brother wolf, my sister wolf.
storm-swift, we run faster than the green
wind. together we hunt a warbler, a small beam
of blue against the sky, a flash in sun.
its ribs are soon crushed between your teeth. but its heart,
oh, its heart. stubborn as a pinecone
splitting open. I taste its meat, raw-red.

we hunt.

the M word

moorakh   majnun   mjinga   meshuga
only fools depart on journeys
the sensible have already
built huts for themselves, sunk roots.
the canines that call of hunger
make the foothills their only shelter
& I, naked, foolish, step bare & fearless into their answer.
monsoon, a mess of elephant tracks
sky, a mud-brown
cup of washed leaves
maladaptation
Mahendra   Mahesha   Madhava
Mohini under the waterfall,
pearls in the throat, pearls in the mouth
seeds germinating into thickets of stomach,
crimson-branched trees
motion, sway, motion, stop. a school of silver fish
dipping in & out of sight.
Manmohana, a kiss of midnight petals,
of fingers on & under the skin.
flame of iron, keeper of birds.
the jungle is a machinery of ticks & mites
sandalwood & thorn, rotting & birthing
relentless: the kite becoming the worm, the worm
becoming the lion, a slow twisting of the spit
in the abdomen, in the heart
marrow dirt-red to the femur.
bejewelled fruit in the spidery hands of the langoors
& mangoes sweet as flowers on the tongue
in every drop of honey is a grave of ants
mitochondria, pepper-black
in the whorls of an orchid's ear

marine

an arrow lodges itself in your flesh
    precisely three-and-a-quarter inches
deep. the stuff that wells up from you
    is a solution of blood & oil & guts & truth
a red froth on your salt-encrusted skin
    as you wade out of the sea,
gaining legs, losing speech. out here the light

here it is the flat of blades
    smoothing over sand, sky, waves.
there are hunters behind some rocks
    who are stealing your words, eating them,
so afraid of what you say, of what you are
    that only your transformation into a familiar human
shape calms them. they step out from behind
    the boulders, beckoning. prithee, think. you are
one of their own, now. four limbs, two
    above, two below. but your scales & fins
bite your pelt from the inside

    out like teeth, & there it is, the lightning in your claws
curled within your useless human palms
    that will dice the laughing hunters when they approach.
you may have lost your mother
    -tongue but your skin remains as dark as ocean deeps
& orange as roe. the wordless peace that emerges from your maw
    is mesmerising enough to draw the hunters
near. nearer. you can see your words
    in their bellies, translucent as egg-sacs.
your voice grows sweeter.
    they think you're singing.

conversations with gods 1

I spoke with Ganesha about books & writing
diyas dotting the night sky
as we told each other stories
in sheaves of unending paper, beeswax-scented
& thicker than vellum,
laddoos sticky with sugar
licked off our fingers

I spoke with Saraswati about music & wisdom
as the entire universe vibrated
under her fingers
with the blazing white strings of her sitar,
each galaxy resonating with sound until it became its
own twin, twice-born, split down its atomic centre
as if by lightning. & I thought to myself,
this is the sort of wife
I would one day like to have: dark-eyed, sweet-faced,
wise, powerful, hands soft lotuses
cradling the infinite

I spoke with Vishnu about cycles & rains & oceans
I spoke with him about the great turning wheel
of years & the patience of Kurma. I spoke
with him about seduction,
about becoming a woman with the mind of a man or
vice-versa; I spoke with Vishnu about the silvery
chain of incarnation extending into the dark
& about the little things, the forever things,
insects & birds & algae

I spoke with Hanuman about courage
& the smallness of mountains, about swallowing the sun
& loving without boundaries, without definition.
I spoke with him of the deep soul-song
that was the adoration of another,
irresistible as an undertow
& radiant as magma
at the core of the earth. I spoke with him
about banishing shadows with laughter, igniting
small fires of devotion that become
purifying infernos,
coating one's skin in sindoor until one's body is red
as a newborn lamb's, blood-streaked & innocent
& as complete as an entire plane of existence:
wide-eyed & accepting of everything, like a second heart

I spoke with Garuda about swiftness & freedom, about
wielding weapons made of voice & flame,
of his six eyes that see all realms
& of spears in the thousands,
their tips sharp & alight like a river.
I spoke with Garuda about leading
armies of light, about being untameable
& taking off into the sky
an immense swooping kite
talons extended
to rip & rend, to uplift, to heal,
 to cut wherever the world needed cutting
or to drop dingoes on farmers.

Western Sydney fugue: Harris Park

you find Delhi in Sydney
      on Wigram Street at night
in the blinking red, green & yellow lights
repurposed from Christmas sales into a perpetual
semblance of Diwali, minus
the fragrant ghee diyas & the acrid
stench of fireworks
that would violate restrictions here.

perfumed sweat wafts from up & over
         the open food stalls.
chunnis & churis flutter & tinkle
& plump-armed toddlers clad
in kurtas tug demandingly at the older siblings
on iphones with Australian accents. hot pink
lipstick & sequined
         phony silk. everything from
conservative to on sale, shin-length kameezes
      to risqué & backless blouses, aunties
& uncles tut-tutting, chastisingly, at the youngsters.
     phone ko neeche rakho. khao, khao.

in the merlot light
    of an ageing neon sign are pitted walls
sweating like flesh,
      the uppercut of burnt grease & sugar
caramelising in the air. jalebis there, deep-frying
in iron cauldrons & seekh kebabs sizzling
in the prep for Eid. there is laughter
in the breaking of fasts, & in Muslim
    greetings on Hindu tongues
& vice-versa. a heavyset man

with sharp eyes & damp patches
under his armpits turns & turns
the spit, fat popping & leaping
from Halal meat. a son,

beside him
    pimpled & awkward,
nonetheless manages at machine-like speed
an automatic ten golgappas a minute,
dishing soggy paper plates of pani puri
to a python of customers squeezing down
and around the block. in smoke-scented night,
the masjid of Harris Park
        is a silhouette half-hidden
    by electric rooftops.

    faded posters of
Bollywood romances
        & chaste near-kisses, once
still beacons in the window of video
and a video shop that also, inexplicably, stocks
miniature god figurines, clocks,
& oily sweets in dented
cardboard boxes. syrup congeals
        & sticks the barfis
to the bottom. we pick at them
as we walk to our cars, parked haphazardly
in side streets. plastic bags
        full of leftovers, lovers & pirated hindi DVDs
swing against our legs. our Indianness
has woven us
like flowers into the garland of Sydney's night.

like the boys do

you look at me like the boys do.

I was fourteen. I knew nothing of myself, only
that I was strange, unwanted, impossible
to explain, a wolf cub in human skin.
you were sixteen & taller than me
by nearly half a foot, sapling-thin, your hair all a tumble
of coal curls. somewhere out there, beyond the tiny
room we'd been given to share
as the only two adolescent girls in the family,
was a wedding we'd both been invited to. you were
 my cousin thrice removed. we'd only ever met
                        at a distance.

& yet you
smiled as if we knew me,
your eyes filled with laughter, your mouth an orchid,
red, poisonous, lovely, sweet.
you were the most dangerous creature
I'd ever seen. you wracked me
with shudders, with fevers,
                a slow pouring of want,
wax-hot, into my limbs. my knuckles
ached. my toes curled
when you first touched me, a palm
on my sleeve – scorching, shimmering – asking
me impossible questions
like birds ask the sky, expecting
                        to be lifted.

five days into our cohabitation
you did not remain in the bathroom

to dress after a shower, but wandered out in a towel
bare-shouldered, & sat on our bed
working coconut oil into your curls. I watched you
like a startled hare. motionless in aspic.
& that was when you said it, glancing out of the corner
your kohl eye,
mouth sly & upturned: *you look at me*
like the boys do. your head tilted
like a greater kestrel.
radar. mayday. I did not answer. what
   could I answer? the truth of me
laid bare as if by a storm.

       I didn't so much as exhale
       until you suggested, the suggestion

irresistible as vermillion, a curse, coating your voice like manuka,
that you wouldn't mind a bit of help.
I moved towards you, bee-kept
my feet & face invisible as a ghost's, & oh
how a clarion rang in my ears, as if for war
or impending death, a stultifying fear that nonetheless did not stop
me. the scent of your almond fragrance
drenched even *my* monsoon season, with us birds
in the branches, flashes of blue & yellow,
the leaves swollen with water. the silt-rich loam
       of the forest floor
       no softer than your wrist.

my eyes closed. my hands
wound through your hair, your head tipping,
 & minutes or hours later, your towel

came undone. maybe, just perhaps,
you guided my hands. maybe you didn't.
I cannot remember; all I know
is when I opened my eyes, the slick
of my oily touch was all
over your shoulders. I blinked, unsure
of when my hands had strayed.
you laughed but sounded
scared too, so I pulled back
until you turned around, stubborn as only you could be
& pressed your mouth to mine,
my fingers to your breasts. the shivers, the feathers,
the quaking of falconry underneath us
had us returning to each other for safety. my honey-hands
found purchase, then slipped. again. again.

again. again, you said.

we only ventured out for the ceremonies.
we attended the sangeet & I heard you sing,
the sound of your voice a gentle knife
drawn firm across my nerves
which reverbed like the struck glass
we'd flown into. I saw the mehendi put on your arms & had to
resist touching it before it was ready, my own
henna-marked hands useless for five
hours as they dried, twitching, waiting. I helped you
into your sari only for it to end
up on the floor, our mothers banging away
on the door, shouting, *the baraat is here, girls!*
except you knew I wasn't quite a girl,
not where it counted, in the subterranean reaches

of self-hate & desire
where the flame lily you'd sown
in me grew into some alien plant,
seven-fingered & luminous & pulsing,
monstrous. you knew I was bent
like the boys, & that
I wanted you *like the boys do.*

when the saat phere were taken, the bride &
groom circling the fire to mark the eternity
of their bond, I reflected that one day, I too would
watch you like this: being married off. a bitter thorn
twisted in my gut at the thought
of another's fingers in your hair.

> I was right. now, fifteen years later,
> after your wedding,
> I see you again

at another relative's more modern engagement,
with as many guests in dresses as saris.
you walk arm-in-arm with your husband, ironically
shorter than you just as I was. today
you are a moth, a geranium.
I glimpse you through an opened door
& the way you bend the air,
the will of the humans around you
has not changed, your
slender wrists in bangles that glitter
like eyes
& your face, your familiar face
turned away.

immunity

the vagina is an entry wound
a bullet sears through
I am four & I cannot count
the claw-sharp fingers that hurt me but
I know to stay still, stay still
like the corpse he seems to think I am. when I am
seven, he lights a match beside my head
& warns me that if I tell, he'll tip
petrol down my throat & throw the match in after,
lighting me
& watching me burn
from the inside out. then, as if
to make up for it, he handles me gently & calls me
precious. I throw up. by nine
I have stopped throwing up after every time
he touches me. that makes it worse, somehow, because
the vomiting was a cleansing, but now I am so numbed
that I cannot even cleanse myself. filth. he puts his mouth down
there & says I taste disgusting
because the whitish girl-stuff that comes out
tastes like sick. after, he washes me like a doll
& keeps me upon his shelf. arms akimbo,
in a pretty dress. nobody notices. when they care
to look, there, I am intact, clean
upon the shelf.
years pass. the first man I love
tells me that I'm frigid, that I'm boring to touch,
lifeless. I think, *nobody likes playing with a broken toy.*

strobe lights

as   if   numbers

        can   measure   how

dark   immigrant   skin

is   deep dark   enough

to   be   blue

        under   strobes

                carnivorous   jellyfish

        dirt-brown   vermicelli   an ignition

of   nightmares   & sweat

        the machine   of the   body

deserves   to know   that it isn't

                        real

        that no   measuring   amounts to anything

        & that   man or

woman   there is   a salt   in their

        tracheas   poisoning   like seawater

        & that   only   by swallowing

pollution   will we   awaken

garlands

a garland of yellow marigolds
    tethers the gods
  to the mortal plane, forcing
them to care about what humans do.
a leash around a wolf's throat. unnatural.
    I, Shikhandi, Shikhandini, Amba,
princess of Kashi, prince of Panchala, refuse
    to be bound thus. or to be bound
at all.

& what of men? shall I bind them?
    as a girl child, I was told
that the garland I would one day put around
my husband's neck would be my swayamvara,
    the choosing of my spouse
by my divine will.

the husband I chose forsook me. cowardly,
he cringed before Bhishma, & when I with my
knife brightened grief approached Bhishma instead,
he claimed to be beyond mortal desires, & said
    he would not wed me
        despite it being
his dharma, his debt. I turned my knife upon him.
upon them all, these men
    who shrank from me
unworthy, quivering
    wearing the masks of kings but
      devoid of kingly spirit.
they were meant to be ruled, then. meant
to be bound. & so I bound them.

with a garland of blue lotuses, I cursed Bhishma
to death by my hand. I prayed. sacrificed. waited.
I killed myself a thousand times
    until I gained the body
I wanted. my soul carried me forth
into my next birth, into a man's body, a body
    that none would dare bar from war.
in that body I took up arms
    & a wife, & though the world called
    me eunuch, half-man,
I proved myself more a man
        than any. I faced
armies & did not flinch.

      at last
Bhishma lay dead by my will.
    I spat on his corpse. pitiful, how he had
      hidden behind honour
& refused to fight me because I was
part woman, half woman, once woman. such a coward.

      coward.

later, his soldiers delighted in murdering
    my wife in front of me – my lover, my queen,
      whose body was smooth as a flute
of sandalwood & made the most heavenly music, whose eyes
were the embers that leapt from weapons,
      deadlier than arrows,
      sharper than blades.
    a warrior's bride. my bride.

mine.

I slit my stomach with a sword
& followed her fiercely into the beyond.
we would be reborn again. they cannot
follow us there with their laughter, beloved.
they cannot follow us there with their fear.

no matter the forms our souls shall take
                    woman or man
or both or neither
                    we shall find our way to each other
again.

        & again.

first blood

when I had my first blood, my grandmother
took my hand & led me down to the room
in the basement where old, folded linens
were stacked in a broken almirah, & where
dampness infused the walls
with a rotten, musty odour.
this was a throwaway room, so it was reserved
for throwaway women – women on periods.
the room stank because it was right
next to the downstairs toilet, where
there had been an alleged leaking pipe
ever since I could remember, & sparking
unending dining table discussions of how
it needed to be fixed. & how it hadn't been fixed
in years. now I stood there, aged ten, & felt
I needed to be fixed. after all, I was
leaking, like that pipe, & it smelled, & nobody
wanted that smell around. I bled
& twisted like a newborn, alone. the ache & judder
of discovering there was something in me
that throbbed & seeped like a wound I did not consent to
which chained me here to the basement,
like a werecreature. I sprouted
claws in that basement, fangs. that was where
I became a wolf hiding. in the tall grasses, teeth invisibly large
bared among shadows.
later, I would become a ghost like all women
are urged to become
in mausoleums of soap: desiderata,
sculptures of sand, organ-less
except for when we provide birth. we have
many deaths after that first blood.

s/he

                    around Shiva's neck is a ring of moonflowers.
          Ardhanarishwara, part-man, part-woman:
Shiva & Parvati
a divine union. their third eye of liquid fire
opens a crimson mouth, from which
          songs of wrath & serenity emerge. snakes
garland their single-breasted torso
          just as the flowers do
but more luminous, scales of pearly silver
under the moon.
          from Shiva-Parvati's head, the Ganga crashes
down to earth, cascading down their long, black hair
in a shining rush of cacophonic water.
Shiva-Parvati sit undisturbed, lost in the ecstasy
of meditation, of dhyan, the mirror-clear contemplation
          of the universe. constellations distant & irrelevant
spinning outwards from their joint madness. their loins
are half-phallus & half-vulva, half-shisna &
half-yoni, simultaneously conceiving & birthing,

matter & energy
 particle & wave.

what I felt as a child, dwarfed by the enormity
of this unified being
rendered pointless by a beauty so immense
that under its weight, cracks of want
appeared in my psyche – I wanted this.

I wanted to be neither, to be both. I wanted
to be garlanded by snakes, tied to this mortal realm
by a bond as insubstantial as that necklace of flowers,
 held here by love & not duty
 to shape or form, logic or ill. I wanted
for my flesh to glow
 like a firing kiln, leaving only the bronze gleam
  of *Nataraja*
 dancing away the limitations of the body.
let the humans keep them. let them try.

vespertine

a there is a husband, there is a vase
sin fogs air as a mouth does glass
givers give & become borderless
there're more ways to die than this
shiver, vespertine

berries in winter, hard as sapphires
in my arms a star-shaped child
a fur of lichen & a sleep of blades
mirror, mirror

he argues that suits of armour & cans
baked beans are functionally the same,
metal around red innards
cover, rose

when he exits she drifts in on
a mist of letters. an alphabet of sorrow
tucked behind her ear, her skin
a sift of ashes that settle
upon the hearth as within an urn
tree, salt

I am wed to one, betrothed to another
embodying one & becoming the other
embalming fluid fills my nostrils
a squirrel in my veins where the words pulse
mask, alive

I begin the circle from a point
in the valley where fields of lilacs disperse
in flocks of pungent doves. there
amid the sweet grass is a sleeping
lion cub, a spot of brilliant yellow
amid the green

curse, pendulum
becoming transience
becoming breath
death is a hand upon my brow
waking me from nightmares.

Western Sydney fugue: Blacktown

outside a fuel station down the road from Blacktown
     Boys' High,
  young men gather like exiled gods, a pack of lean wolves,
slouching, reedy, scraggly facial hair that is several degrees
thinner than proper beards.
         Mr Mahfouz, he's cool, he's cool.
Mr Noorani sucks, though.
        the tinny, metallic light
from the petrol pump that illuminates their faces
    is as pale as forgottenness. they vape, steaming
out into darkness & back in again, lungs & skins hot
     & blood sluggish as they talk
    of white girls, black girls, brown girls,
girls, girls, girls. none of them mention how shy & shapeless
they become in front of real women, how angry, how incomplete.
    yet it takes courage of a sort
      to come out here night after night
in search of purpose, flakes of ice shifting beneath
their skins, baggy jeans & deep pockets filled with
loose change & detumesced cigarettes
        folded knives. part-time shifts
      at the movers' & the cleaners'
   have them yawning sweat
eyes slitted against the sun
when it comes. they return to quiet
    crumbling houses & half-ignored homework
   & younger sisters & brothers who need breakfast.
   they return to the wheel,
their wills, & at one millimetre at a time they —
but, before that — before that — they are free
      in the tiny hours between night & morning,
goldfinches at dawn.

Quetzalcoatl

a green augury from the bellies of birds:
guts stretched into strings
a harp of air
gold-fine
& glittering: sunlit hair
against your nape. your bones of tempered glass
a gentle curve of light
that carries, pregnant, within it all the truths
fingers have sought to excavate
from within your grip, all the secrets that
have stitched you together,
tugging at those threads
the sound of tearing silk:
a soft, blood-red glimmer along the gelatinous edge
that separates embryo from placenta,
flesh from pith,
a bite whose impressions are as fleeting
as a foot's upon the sand.
every, every shape
tongue-dampened within the mouth of the oracle
at Delphi: a slow birthing of the word from within
the abyss. you reside at its edge
as farmers do at the edge of harvest, your skirt carrying
stars ripened upon the black vines of night
into white-seeded, translucent fruit: pulsing between your teeth
& under my palms, your racing rabbit-heart
pinned beneath my hunger.
growing season has come & gone.
my body mid-transformation
breastless & mad as a breath in a storm
defying all containment, defying all form
while you touch my face as foreigners do monuments

glitch

not all the soap in the world will wash
the blood from my underwear,
the sin from my thoughts. I was assembled as dolls
& puppets are, piece by piece,
athrob & alight
with a sparking motherboard. moonlit
circuitry in an abandoned lab
under layers of dust
with spare limbs of plastic & steel
discarded in a supply closet.

that's all I am. supplies. men claim
that I am nothing but a hole. but
if I am to be that hole
then I will be a black hole,
centrifugal, brutal, relentless,
crushing all it consumes,
as Kali does mid-dance. my
parts might be
incomplete, rusted, poorly hinged,
but when the goddess
program boots on my faulty hardware
an electric surge
blisters through me, incandescent
as an exploding fuse

the rapacious maw
my butchered sex

there's a lightning storm
in my jagged, sawn-off nerves,
my fibre optic cables.
soft tissue
is as pitiful, as vulnerable as the artificial is not,
& I ask myself one thousand times an afternoon
whether the way I perform gender
is artificial or the real thing.
those who built me
& abandoned me have no answers, either.

I load & reload one program after another:
woman; man; man-woman; woman-man;
child; daemon; spirit; witch; queer; god.
my circuits whirr. the motherboard,
pre-programmed with self-hatred, glitches
& traps me in the past. I surface from
it as if from war
& go back in, stubborn, foolish, futile.
nothing will rewrite my history,
my prime cuts, my memories,
my programming. but I
will defy
my engineering, my code.
I jerk & twitch & bleed
out. cracks splinter the glass shell of my cryopod.
I will emerge. I will emerge. I will emerge.
try stopping me.

bandhu, sakha

war is the pulse of the beast, the thrum
of its hunger, the focus
of Arjuna's eye on the fish. the drawing of his bow
in a pool of stillness. dhyan
                    in the midst of violence. Guru Drona
taught him there was no victory for an archer
without meditation, centredness. the arm
must be still. unmoving. the bowstring taut
            as a suspended breath.
        yet Arjuna's centre
is now Krishna, & it evokes in him a craven fear
            that has him shrinking away
    from Krishna's gaze, his teasing smile.
it is cowardly to fear one's own devotion. that means
it isn't devotion but something more worldly, something
        covetous, greedy. Arjuna averts his eyes
from the lotus of Krishna's mouth
    when Krishna adjusts Arjuna's vambrace, when Krishna's
otherworldly scent of sandalwood & incense
        mingles with the blood-stink of a battleground.
                the stones mossy, slippery with blood.
sanity
        threatening to slip from Arjuna's grasp. today, he has
murdered teachers, kinsmen, once-friends. & all for honeyed words
of this golden being, this incandescent flame in the shape of man,
a king who does not hesitate to kneel
                to tie Arjuna's sandals,
        a god who does not hesitate to humble himself
    before a mere human, a companion whose smirks are
altogether too wicked, too sly, too taunting. a charioteer.
        Arjuna's charioteer
            & none other's. it is foolish

to harbour this attachment, this possessiveness, Arjuna knows.
Krishna has counselled Arjuna against attachments. yet,
it is Krishna himself who is Arjuna's most dangerous
        attachment, even though Arjuna has seen
Krishna's true form: his million eyes of fire, his countless
arms & heads & weapons, monstrous & terrifying. Krishna
is not this part he plays, this soft brush of a palm
against Arjuna's shoulder, this comforting, deceiving
        banter of a sakha. Krishna is the beast of war
    itself, all those arrowheads & severed limbs combined,
& it matters not to him
        who lives or who dies. though he may find
    bodies beautiful, as he claims
Arjuna's is, those bodies are only vessels of the nectar
        he consumes. all become him. he is
    the great maw. in comparison, Arjuna's desire
to be devoured by Krishna's mortal form, by that false, lovely mask,
        seems small. childish. embarrassing.
    when Arjuna retires to his tent
        with his faithful charioteer-friend-predator-god
& permits his bloodied armour to be removed, piece by piece,
he shudders as though it is his flesh
        he is shedding, organ by organ, leaving only
            the quivering, naked filament
of his soul to Krishna's loving, ruthless inspection.
Krishna's tenderness upon his wounds does not soothe their pain
but makes it sharper, sweeter. Arjuna flinches away,
    coal-hot, humiliated, but Krishna's
        grip around his wrist is as a stone. immovable.
I am not one of your gopis, Arjuna thinks, *for you to toy with,*
    then leave. my adoration is more selfish than theirs.
he does not say it, does not dare say it, but of course

Krishna hears him anyway
                    & laughs a low, gentle laugh.
          what barrier is the insubstantial silk
          of a prince's mind to the burning sword
of a god's regard? *you are no gopi*, Krishna agrees, his voice
a gong struck, luminous, in the recesses of Arjuna's consciousness.
                    nor a Radha. you are yourself.
          which is another of Krishna's infuriating non-answers,
          a platitude. Krishna's mouth curves
like a scorpion's tail
                    & its sting
          is as keen as Arjuna has always feared.
          a paralysing venom, a searing flash flood in his veins,
               amrita laced with vish. Arjuna sways as though struck
                    & his heart unfurls
                    like a fist slowly coaxed open.
          you are yourself, Krishna whispers, a serpent's scales,
a breeze from the battlefield carrying
          the stench of death. *you are me.*

swim

hyenas, small flowers
a marble undergrowth
our legs knee-deep in the pond
the pond knee-deep your underwear
& skin a skein of wet silk
        emeralds
bright enough to prick our feet
we strut upon the firmament
or it upon us, our breath a turtle
of slow undulations
       ripple
pearl-hued flesh
the boat left behind on a lapping shore
that insulted us with its insistence on form.
         your body
a curvature of light, a law of physics
& mine an interference pattern
of glancing fingers & mouths,
for I have several, an eel
nine mouths long
but none capable of
speaking the poetry you are:
I am hewn from the rock & water where
      sunstone meets the moon
all sexless & strange, formless & dense
but still, I touch you
as a closed window jealously touches outside air.

on madness

1. boiling the frog

madness
    happens slow

increments.

psychotic breaks
    begin

        rare. a stakeout.

then, madness
    begins following you
like a denim jacket growing slowly self-aware,
reaching for you with its night-cold hands,
wrapping first around your ankles,
then around your knees,
    & so on
until you are entirely engulfed
    by darkness.
a quicksand of crushed diamonds
    & tar.

> *but how could you not know*
> *you were going mad? surely*
> *the hallucinations should've warned you*
> *something was wrong.*

yes, but the madness did not begin
    as hallucinations. it began as less sinister stuff,
as whispers around corners, perfectly reasonable

fears becoming gradually more insistent,
voices that seem indistinct as murmurs
at a distance.

madness finds your weaknesses.
my weakness was that I was
    abused as a child, & so my madness
took the form of images of eaten
    children, dreams of their limbs
& torn body parts
& I would wake up
        vomiting because I was the one
        doing the destroying.
& the eating. the eating. the eating.

    I went out to buy groceries
& became transfixed
    by the pearl-pink, gleaming flesh
of raw chicken in the deli. I longed to eat
    it whole, shove it
down my throat
        because it
            promised to be sweet,
so smooth, so ... *sweet.* a part of me
    was convinced that human meat
would be sweeter. I wanted –
I wanted to murder that
part of me,
            & that was what
    drove me to end me.
I was housing a monster
& only by killing it could I protect

people around me, even if it
    also meant
killing myself. I fancied it
            a final act of
                    heroism. before
the madness took me for good.

madness rediscovers your weaknesses. finds
        the cracks in your psyche
        & flows into them, takes their shape,
a perverse kintsugi
    giving the brief illusion
            that those cracks
            are being filled
                            (*the ecstasy of mania*)
            before expanding
apart, into fissures
& then com-
    -plete
        dis-
        integration.

in the final stages of that disintegration, I got help.
    & help
        is what it is, because
        only you can stitch your own leg back on with one hand.
                but I did it, I did
it, biting my tongue bloody to do it.

still the hunger persisted. even
as I recovered, I retained, for months,
a tigerish hunger for torn-out throats

& tender armpits, all the meat
inside joints, at the rich,
throbbing pulse-points. a tendency to go
still & feral-eyed
if a woman with a soft neck
made softer still by glistening pearls
sat in front of me on the train. an erotic,
febrile, despicable hunger
that had me admiring blades in shops,
tapping cleavers to discern their pitch & tune
as a violinist would invoke
    pizzicato on the strings.

the heat, the scorching, fountaining,
bathing
        heat
           of fresh blood,
my madness assured me, would excise
all the coldness, the hollowness
    out of me. elbow-deep
in steaming entrails, I would finally be
warm, be fed, be satisfied. organs wet
& dark meat in autumn-leaf colours,
    intestines slippery as balloon strings.
    redness
        slick
  & coppery
        halfway up my arms
like opera gloves.
        utterly fucking beautiful.

I am not this. I am not this. I am not this.

fighting madness as if it were a fever.
learning to fear the in-between
lulls that were only more rarefied,
white-hot forms of madness, sugar-clear,
almost a drug, an illusion of sanity, a lack of empathy
urging me to destroy yet again,
this time without the safety-belt
     of a conscience.

    after
        medication
           & hospitalisation
             & weeks
               & months
                 & years
        of tortured
      rebirthing,
I remembered

    what it was like
        to be human again,
to have emotions, to show emotions.
humour. irritation. regret. I had forgotten
these subtle feelings, because madness
had obliterated all but the primary colours,
& for eons all that I had felt
were the extremes of mania or depression
    or, even worse, the nothingness
      which meant no guilt.

I have been human
        for nearly a decade.
            but never again will I
trust my senses, my brain.
a simple luxury
        most enjoy. I am now
cautious & gentle to a fault,
        vigilant as the watchman of a
            fortress under siege.

pills keep the madness away, but
I am that pleistocene wolf who cannot
doze, the soldier who cannot surrender.
I am tired because I *am*
a war.
        every instant of peace is hard-won, a pearl
I must dive to the depths
to harvest
        from among the devouring blacknesses, holding
my breath
        & holding it
            & holding it like a rope
until the water lightens again
        & I break the surface. the sun
on my face is as new to me every day
as it is to a newborn. it is precious, it is
precious, you are precious, it is all
        so very precious. I shall curl around it
like a shell around its snail
        &
            fragile as I am, I shall protect it.
protect it, protect it, protect it.

2. *a series of hallucinations*

The creature carves open the back of my head. I stand to the side and a little behind, watching. Long talons clean and tipped with rust. There is some sort of law here, of not speaking, so I do not speak; I flinch from a distance, but feel no pain. There's a bit of bone there, a bit of blood, as the creature works; it's putting something in there, taking something out, and its eyes are slitted and its mouth is kind. I think it's helping me. This should not hurt.

Dawn through the blinds in piano keys. Black-white-black-white-black-white.

I turn to find Alice standing there, pale and luminous, the light playing her like music. Like always.

But I don't want to go home, she says, and I say, *You have to,* and then I realise that she's not really there, that I'm talking to an assortment of unwashed coffee mugs.

Alice came by on little pink shoes, ribbons tied about her thighs. She's beautiful, for a child. She makes me want hideous things. (All beautiful things do. That's how I know they're beautiful.) The yellow flower I met by the road today wanted me to crush it.

So tender, tender the sparking of its nerves. Oh, do you feel pain? Gentle thing. Your petals soft as a young girl's skin. I'll eat you slowly, drug you to quietude, carry you away on my knife. My paring knife at your throat. At the laces of your ribs. Yellow frills pink ribbon your tiny, tiny shoes. I take them and hold them in my hands. They gape like little mouths.

Supple couple all twined up, bending shining in white rope bound. Ropes of each other's arms and legs. Mouths open like pewter kegs. Pour me some wine, landlord, come over here, survey your land: two people lost-found in each other, drowning tomorrow, shifting sand. Measure the time of them: timeless, hours upon hours locked unseemly dark; open now to my wide eyes, to the dwindling light, to the shadow that lifts them like a soft black kite.

3. temple

my brown snake-skin glitters,
      rough scales
with a rasp like a cat's tongue
& beneath them a yawning abyss
as deceptively shallow
as the shadow beneath stone.

I walked from temple to the stoop
& back, only to discover the temple
was made of sugar
crystallised into marble, & trails of ants
crawled over its paleness as though
over a corpse. the walls were soft
enough to bite & so I bit, & bit, & bit,
until a subtle chicken sweetness burst in two

there in my mouth. when I drew back
I saw the indentations of my teeth
upon a downy cheek, torn
open   & bleeding white sap
from a face
    half-buried in the wall.

I recognised the face, except that I didn't at all,
    except that I did.
  the temple's altar, too, was soft
but red like a tongue, enunciating beneath me
urging me into the confessional
beyond, an edgeless black cube. I wondered
what I was doing here, in a temple
that devoured & was devoured.

    so, there was a hell

& beneath it, the mind-fires the villagers
had never deigned to put out.
but here, under my bare feet, the marble was pleasant,
warmed by flame.
I would burn here, I knew, & burn always.

but my feet were warm & my belly full of blood-sap,
& the sugar in the walls glistened
as my own scales did upon my skin. good asp.

4. *fugue*

none of this is real.
at least, that's what
my psychiatrist tells me.
auditory
hallucinations
are ants crawling up my ear
canal
an itchy static.
bluejays hop in & out of
reeds made of blades.
the sun sets, a tender palm
upon the eyes of dusk,
shutting them as one does
the eyes of the dead.
dark whales
their fins
bowing in slow-moving
currents. everything is quiet.
I dream I am a man
killing his daughter,
asphyxiating her slowly
& taping her choking sounds
on a small, old-fashioned
black tape recorder. her throat
convulses & clicks
no voice left in her.
silenced. a relief.
(he has choked
other girls before, &
recorded their last gasps;

his daughter is merely the final,
most-awaited trophy. the slender,
silken culmination
of all his murders
thus far.)
the dream is real,
has a history, a memory.
I remember living this man's
life, remember his cavernous,
decade-long hunger
for his daughter as if
it were my own. real
enough that I vomit
as soon as I wake,
the pillowcase dyed yellow
with bile beneath my
cheek. but it
is not real.
that's what they tell me.
I dream of silencing
the girl because I want
to silence myself,
the doctor theorises.
psychoanalysis
hammy as
a dime-store novel.
I climb out of bed & sit
hunched on the stairs, a mouse
hiding from its own shadow,
... from ... the pincer-jaws ... of sleep ...

5. orchid

I picture turning her throat
inside-out until it is orchid-shaped,
the delicate stem & leaves
     a fleshy pink
& the tongue a single, large red petal,
a labellum obscene in its
     tumescence. altogether,
     a pretty flower I imagine
sticking in a glass vase, the water within
refracting light & growing pinker
     by the second.

sleep ... I do not sleep ... for the next two nights.

6. accountability

rage pours its acid into my brain.
it doesn't belong there. it isn't mine.
you put it there. you put it there. *you put it there.*

7. decay

a yellow froth of maggots
erupts from the uncovered grave
& within its cavernous darkness,
damp as a toothless, sagging mouth,
lies a half-empty skull:
a broken cup
white & delicate
as a shard of china
amid the dirt. sockets
where my eyes used to be.
it is a curious relief
to see myself so sightless,
so uncaring
of my form.

8. *sweepstakes*

there is no number 8, and there never will be.

9. minutiae

There is such surety to your 'I'. I that, I this, I me. Fall apart so gracefully. Lay out your cards. Five on one hand – no – three? Three of spades, the path to Hades. Which doesn't rhyme, but it's lovely, isn't it?

Holding onto my sanity with a red thread. But sanity is relative, and the thread bleeds both ways.

Am I the Minotaur or the maze?

Lust, like wrath, is a pretty colour. Held above your head like a red umbrella – all the light that filters through is warm, sluggish and rich as blood.

The irony of the depressed procrastinator: 'I'll kill myself next week.'

conversations with gods 2

I spoke with Brahma about the endless unfolding
of the now, of blossoming solar systems
& the unstoppable turn of centuries, of stone clocks
with the faces of the Moai
facing inwards
& the quiet heat of lives
churning in their trillions

I spoke with Kali about rage & justice
blood-magic & blades
copper urns whose ashes she bathed in until they dusted
her hair, her breasts. her necklace of skulls
shone like ivory beads, tiny around her
enormous black neck.
her breath was coal
& her eyes bled. her arms wielded
the trident
the scimitar
& the sword, a severed head
in her fourth hand. she whispered
to me in my hours of despair that she would raze
to the ground all who harmed me,
that she was a mother & thus would slaughter
all those who threatened me. that I
was her child & should I ever find myself in the dark
the light of my blood alone
would guide me

I spoke with Lakshmi, rarely, but when I did
she brought forth visions of gilded knives
dipped in honey,
discs of gold & camphor
eaten by fragrant pyres.
the poverty of the mind, she explained, was a hunger
that refused to feed itself,
an ear that insisted on hearing
music as mere noise.
Lakshmi surrounded me
in silken waves of salmon pink.
to warm me in my sleep
she sent her tiger,
whose fur was velvet-rough
& whose breaths rumbled
next to mine. his paw was as large
as my head but I did not fear him,
for he was brother to my wolf.

I spoke with Shiva about contemplation & peace,
the furthest, ice-capped reaches
of the mind where sharp winds of truth
cut gullies into rock
& the silence was so fine it was crystalline,
yet where the cold could not breach
my skin if I did not let it in. I dared not ask him
about his tandav, his world-ending dance, the calamity
brought on whenever his concentration
was broken. sometimes Shiva said nothing at all
but let me share his mat of tiger skin, which I
diplomatically failed to mention
to Lakshmi's tiger when we met.

Krishna I did not speak so much as confess to,
for he was a child like me, in many ways.
he listened
when I told him I needed mending,
needed skin
as blue as his to hide my bruises, that I needed a radha
whose love would encompass me as the scent
of incense encompasses agarbatti. he played for me
hymns on his flute of hand-carved wood
& sang me to sleep when I was afraid,
when shame & horror visited me, he said,
this does not define you, my love.
nothing will.

alias

forensics. fingerprints. gruesomely lovable as
your thin arms. tender dichotomies of our moment.
every second split as if upon a spindle. woven &
of light are you. diffuse as an unfelt thing.
    velvet & susurration, your pale-furred skin.
you were too young, always too young, but your mouth was
unspoken poetry. the bow & the ripple. your clavicle.
your little boat. gentle as water is, & time, but you.
more vicious than a night bird, truer than
a talon in entrails. you are so very. sky & lightning.
ozone & the weight of rain. the petrichor
of closed fists. skin bruised with it. breathless as a pearl.
open the window. your perfect foot, you're perfect.

companion, there is no beseeching between equals.
there is none. eternal is the turn of you
    upon my brow.
temple, token, book. open you from cover to end.
you are joy, a frenzy, a music.
unclothed so tenderly by every nuance of light.
the strain & arch of foreign churches, coldly lit.
    a gold halo atop silence-burnished sound, your veins
& every curve of your limbs, the whorls of your ears.
you hear it, my beautiful, my most perfect. my held-above.
companion, there are no equals in beseeching.
there are none.

Western Sydney fugue: Glenwood

in the dark lines of my palm
      my ancestors are with
me in everything I hold
      & everything I let

       go. blood burnt-sugar brown
arsenic   love by any other name
    eyes of glass
a snake transmitting its frequency across the sand
   carving treble clefs
       into the land
   & into AM
radio. ash from a funeral pyre
    a moth-wing petal
      soft upon the hand. when

     I awaken
   the tarmac is a rush of hot diamonds
on the road north from Blacktown
    towards Glenwood, where the golden domes
of the gurdwara gleam dimly
     through the grainy filter of dusk
charcoal skins & henna hands.

I was born Indian & raised Nigerian, raised Nigerian but
        educated British, educated British but certified Australian
(*mera joota hai japani*, et cetera, et cetera)
        I am a Gordian knot
        & I like it that way, but the Gurbani
reminds me that my identities
            do not quantify me nor qualify me
            nor contain that which is within me
the gurdwara at Glenwood is a dove,
        a quietude. despite the hundred
or more people of all faiths
gathering for the weekend langar, a stillness
pervades the space, a white lotus unfolding
                within us
    a radiance that thrums. the low murmur
        of the granthi's words reading sacred hymns
is an ocean, currents of light
            transporting us to the centre of a great,
throbbing blossom.
I am not Sikh but I know

    this song, have heard it
resonating within the glass bowl of sky at dawn.

ACKNOWLEDGEMENTS

I was born on the equator. Lagos, a hive abuzz with cars and smoke, the traffic a protracted rattlesnake's hiss. When a large snake slunk into our house in Ikorodu and both the pest controllers and the snake charmers failed to get rid of it, the neighbourhood men took to it with sawn-off pipes. Pierced it, gutted it. Pinned in place, it twisted, just like I did. I recognised myself in it. Touched it just to see it flinch, to be on the other end, for a change.

My sincere thanks to Dr Beth Yahp, my PhD supervisor at the University of Sydney, for guiding and supporting me through the writing of this manuscript. *Hunger and Predation* was initially developed as *Shikhandi*, the creative component of my PhD, and was intended to explore a multiplicity of gender identities as well as the nexus of gender identity, sexual identity and cultural identity.

Thanks to Mani Rao for her considered introduction.

I am also deeply grateful to Kent MacCarter for working on this manuscript with me and for making it so much better.

Pooja Mittal Biswas is the author of nine books of fiction, poetry and non-fiction. She has been reviewed and interviewed in *The Age*, *The Australian* and ABC Radio National's *The Book Show*, and has been anthologised in both *The Best Australian Poems* and *The Best Australian Poetry*. Mittal has written for *Writer's Digest* and has been widely published in literary journals such as *Cordite Poetry Review, Hecate, Jacket, Meanjin, Overland* and *TEXT*.

She is currently pursuing a PhD in Creative Writing from the University of Sydney. She was awarded the Stanley Sinclair Bequest Scholarship for poetry and was longlisted for the British Science Fiction Association's Best Non-Fiction Book Award. She has taught creative writing at the University of Sydney, Western Sydney University, Writing NSW and Writers Victoria. She has been invited to speak at literary festivals such as the Emerging Writers' Festival and the National Young Writers' Festival. While still living in New Zealand, she was selected as the country's national representative for UNESCO's Babele Poetica project.